LIFE
ULTIMATE PLANNER

January - March 2023
Q1

THIS PLANNER BELONGS TO

_____
NAME

_____
EMAIL

_____
CELL

GET STARTED

The Life Ultimate Planner is designed for anyone who wants to make their life count for more. It is a tool, a road map to be successful. The Life Ultimate Planner will help you create alignment with your life priorities. You will have increased confidence with decision making. You will find yourself in the drivers seat of life, feel organized and respected as an inspirational leader. It is the planner designed for people who love to plan, as well as those who need help planning. Start slow, set your own pace, but commit to it and watch your life become more manageable and productive.

Copyright©2023 Cheryl Jackson. All rights reserved.

ISBN: 978-1-960130-00-6

www.LiveLifeFullyCoaching.com

CONTENTS

2023 Calendar..4
2024 Calendar..5

January 2023 Calendar...6
January Master Success Actions................................8
January Weekly and Daily Pages...............................10
January Income Tracker.......................................60
January Expense Tracker......................................61
January Savings Tracker......................................62
January Monthly Progress.....................................63

February 2023 Calendar.......................................64
February Master Success Actions..............................66
February Weekly and Daily Pages..............................68
February Income Tracker.....................................108
February Expense Tracker....................................109
February Savings Tracker....................................110
February Monthly Progress...................................111

March 2023 Calendar...112
March Master Success Actions................................114
March Weekly and Daily Pages................................116
March Income Tracker..156
March Expense Tracker.......................................157
March Savings Tracker.......................................158
March Monthly Progress......................................159

Books to Read...160
Wish List...161
Notes Pages...162
Index...182

2023 CALENDAR

JANUARY

M	T	W	T	F	S	S
						1
2	3	4	5	6	7	8
9	10	11	12	13	14	15
16	17	18	19	20	21	22
23	24	25	26	27	28	29
30	31					

FEBRUARY

M	T	W	T	F	S	S
		1	2	3	4	5
6	7	8	9	10	11	12
13	14	15	16	17	18	19
20	21	22	23	24	25	26
27	28					

MARCH

M	T	W	T	F	S	S
		1	2	3	4	5
6	7	8	9	10	11	12
13	14	15	16	17	18	19
20	21	22	23	24	25	26
27	28	29	30	31		

APRIL

M	T	W	T	F	S	S
					1	2
3	4	5	6	7	8	9
10	11	12	13	14	15	16
17	18	19	20	21	22	23
24	25	26	27	28	29	30

MAY

M	T	W	T	F	S	S
1	2	3	4	5	6	7
8	9	10	11	12	13	14
15	16	17	18	19	20	21
22	23	24	25	26	27	28
29	30	31				

JUNE

M	T	W	T	F	S	S
			1	2	3	4
5	6	7	8	9	10	11
12	13	14	15	16	17	18
19	20	21	22	23	24	25
26	27	28	29	30		

JULY

M	T	W	T	F	S	S
					1	2
3	4	5	6	7	8	9
10	11	12	13	14	15	16
17	18	19	20	21	22	23
24	25	26	27	28	29	30
31						

AUGUST

M	T	W	T	F	S	S
	1	2	3	4	5	6
7	8	9	10	11	12	13
14	15	16	17	18	19	20
21	22	23	24	25	26	27
28	29	30	31			

SEPTEMBER

M	T	W	T	F	S	S
				1	2	3
4	5	6	7	8	9	10
11	12	13	14	15	16	17
18	19	20	21	22	23	24
25	26	27	28	29	30	

OCTOBER

M	T	W	T	F	S	S
						1
2	3	4	5	6	7	8
9	10	11	12	13	14	15
16	17	18	19	20	21	22
23	24	25	26	27	28	29
30	31					

NOVEMBER

M	T	W	T	F	S	S
		1	2	3	4	5
6	7	8	9	10	11	12
13	14	15	16	17	18	19
20	21	22	23	24	25	26
27	28	29	30			

DECEMBER

M	T	W	T	F	S	S
				1	2	3
4	5	6	7	8	9	10
11	12	13	14	15	16	17
18	19	20	21	22	23	24
25	26	27	28	29	30	31

2024 CALENDAR

JANUARY

M	T	W	T	F	S	S
1	2	3	4	5	6	7
8	9	10	11	12	13	14
15	16	17	18	19	20	21
22	23	24	25	26	27	28
29	30	31				

FEBRUARY

M	T	W	T	F	S	S
			1	2	3	4
5	6	7	8	9	10	11
12	13	14	15	16	17	18
19	20	21	22	23	24	25
26	27	28	29			

MARCH

M	T	W	T	F	S	S
				1	2	3
4	5	6	7	8	9	10
11	12	13	14	15	16	17
18	19	20	21	22	23	24
25	26	27	28	29	30	31

APRIL

M	T	W	T	F	S	S
1	2	3	4	5	6	7
8	9	10	11	12	13	14
15	16	17	18	19	20	21
22	23	24	25	26	27	28
29	30					

MAY

M	T	W	T	F	S	S
		1	2	3	4	5
6	7	8	9	10	11	12
13	14	15	16	17	18	19
20	21	22	23	24	25	26
27	28	29	30	31		

JUNE

M	T	W	T	F	S	S
					1	2
3	4	5	6	7	8	9
10	11	12	13	14	15	16
17	18	19	20	21	22	23
24	25	26	27	28	29	30

JULY

M	T	W	T	F	S	S
1	2	3	4	5	6	7
8	9	10	11	12	13	14
15	16	17	18	19	20	21
22	23	24	25	26	27	28
29	30	31				

AUGUST

M	T	W	T	F	S	S
			1	2	3	4
5	6	7	8	9	10	11
12	13	14	15	16	17	18
19	20	21	22	23	24	25
26	27	28	29	30	31	

SEPTEMBER

M	T	W	T	F	S	S
						1
2	3	4	5	6	7	8
9	10	11	12	13	14	15
16	17	18	19	20	21	22
23	24	25	26	27	28	29
30						

OCTOBER

M	T	W	T	F	S	S
	1	2	3	4	5	6
7	8	9	10	11	12	13
14	15	16	17	18	19	20
21	22	23	24	25	26	27
28	29	30	31			

NOVEMBER

M	T	W	T	F	S	S
				1	2	3
4	5	6	7	8	9	10
11	12	13	14	15	16	17
18	19	20	21	22	23	24
25	26	27	28	29	30	

DECEMBER

M	T	W	T	F	S	S
						1
2	3	4	5	6	7	8
9	10	11	12	13	14	15
16	17	18	19	20	21	22
23	24	25	26	27	28	29
30	31					

JANUARY

MONDAY	TUESDAY	WEDNESDAY	THURSDAY
2	3	4	5
9	10	11	12
16	17	18	19
23	24	25	26
30	31		

GOALS

2023

FRIDAY	SATURDAY	SUNDAY	NOTES
6	7	8	
13	14	15	
20	21	22	
27	28	29	

NOTES

MASTER SUCCESS ACTIONS
JANUARY 2023

List 4 life areas and your goals to focus on this month:

1.

2.

3.

4.

Use this master task list for the big action steps you will commit to do this month. They will accomplish the goals you set to improve your life in the 4 areas of focus. Your daily tasks will be the small steps to accomplish these bigger steps.

DONE	SUCCESS ACTIONS

NOTES

WEEKLY PLANNER

QUOTE OF THE WEEK:

MONDAY 2

TUESDAY 3

WEDNESDAY 4

THURSDAY 5

FRIDAY 6

SATURDAY 7

SUNDAY 8

SUCCESS FOCUS:

PRIORITIES / GOALS

○ _____
○ _____
○ _____
○ _____
○ _____
○ _____
○ _____
○ _____
○ _____

NOTES

JANUARY 2 – 8, 2023

	BREAKFAST	LUNCH	DINNER	SNACKS
M				
T				
W				
T				
F				
S				
S				

SHOPPING LIST:

NOTES

MONDAY
JANUARY 2023

2

TODAY'S PRAYER & FOCUS:

SCHEDULE

TIME	APPOINTMENT

PRIORITIES / GOALS

- ◯
- ◯
- ◯
- ◯
- ◯
- ◯
- ◯
- ◯
- ◯
- ◯

NOTES & SCRIBBLES

HABITS – 1 NEW PER MONTH
1.
2.
3.

TODAY I'M GRATEFUL FOR

3

TUESDAY
JANUARY 2023

TODAY'S PRAYER & FOCUS:

SCHEDULE

TIME	APPOINTMENT

PRIORITIES / GOALS

- ○
- ○
- ○
- ○
- ○
- ○
- ○
- ○
- ○
- ○

NOTES & SCRIBBLES

HABITS – 1 NEW PER MONTH

1.
2.
3.

TODAY I'M GRATEFUL FOR

WEDNESDAY
JANUARY 2023

4

TODAY'S PRAYER & FOCUS:

SCHEDULE

TIME	APPOINTMENT

PRIORITIES / GOALS

- ○
- ○
- ○
- ○
- ○
- ○
- ○
- ○
- ○
- ○

NOTES & SCRIBBLES

HABITS – 1 NEW PER MONTH

1.
2.
3.

TODAY I'M GRATEFUL FOR

5

THURSDAY
JANUARY 2023

TODAY'S PRAYER & FOCUS:

SCHEDULE

TIME	APPOINTMENT

PRIORITIES / GOALS

- ○
- ○
- ○
- ○
- ○
- ○
- ○
- ○
- ○
- ○

NOTES & SCRIBBLES

HABITS – 1 NEW PER MONTH

1.
2.
3.

TODAY I'M GRATEFUL FOR

FRIDAY
JANUARY 2023

6

TODAY'S PRAYER & FOCUS:

SCHEDULE

TIME	APPOINTMENT

PRIORITIES / GOALS

- ○
- ○
- ○
- ○
- ○
- ○
- ○
- ○
- ○
- ○

NOTES & SCRIBBLES

HABITS – 1 NEW PER MONTH

1.
2.
3.

TODAY I'M GRATEFUL FOR

7

SATURDAY
JANUARY 2023

TODAY'S PRAYER & FOCUS:

SCHEDULE

TIME	APPOINTMENT

PRIORITIES / GOALS

- ○
- ○
- ○
- ○
- ○
- ○
- ○
- ○
- ○
- ○

NOTES & SCRIBBLES

HABITS — 1 NEW PER MONTH

1.
2.
3.

TODAY I'M GRATEFUL FOR

SUNDAY
JANUARY 2023

8

TODAY'S PRAYER & FOCUS:

SCHEDULE

TIME	APPOINTMENT

PRIORITIES / GOALS

○
○
○
○
○
○
○
○
○
○

NOTES & SCRIBBLES

HABITS – 1 NEW PER MONTH

1.
2.
3.

TODAY I'M GRATEFUL FOR

WEEKLY PLANNER

QUOTE OF THE WEEK:

MONDAY 9
TUESDAY 10
WEDNESDAY 11
THURSDAY 12
FRIDAY 13
SATURDAY 14
SUNDAY 15

SUCCESS FOCUS:

PRIORITIES / GOALS

- ○
- ○
- ○
- ○
- ○
- ○
- ○
- ○
- ○
- ○

NOTES

JANUARY 9 – 15, 2023

	BREAKFAST	LUNCH	DINNER	SNACKS
M				
T				
W				
T				
F				
S				
S				

SHOPPING LIST:

NOTES

MONDAY
JANUARY 2023

9

TODAY'S PRAYER & FOCUS:

SCHEDULE

TIME	APPOINTMENT

PRIORITIES / GOALS

○
○
○
○
○
○
○
○
○
○

NOTES & SCRIBBLES

HABITS – 1 NEW PER MONTH
1.
2.
3.

TODAY I'M GRATEFUL FOR

10

TUESDAY
JANUARY 2023

TODAY'S PRAYER & FOCUS:

SCHEDULE

TIME	APPOINTMENT

PRIORITIES / GOALS

- ◯
- ◯
- ◯
- ◯
- ◯
- ◯
- ◯
- ◯
- ◯
- ◯

NOTES & SCRIBBLES

HABITS – 1 NEW PER MONTH

1.
2.
3.

TODAY I'M GRATEFUL FOR

WEDNESDAY
JANUARY 2023
11

TODAY'S PRAYER & FOCUS:

SCHEDULE

TIME	APPOINTMENT

PRIORITIES / GOALS

- ○
- ○
- ○
- ○
- ○
- ○
- ○
- ○
- ○
- ○

NOTES & SCRIBBLES

HABITS – 1 NEW PER MONTH
1.
2.
3.

TODAY I'M GRATEFUL FOR

12

THURSDAY
JANUARY 2023

TODAY'S PRAYER & FOCUS:

SCHEDULE

TIME	APPOINTMENT

PRIORITIES / GOALS

- ○
- ○
- ○
- ○
- ○
- ○
- ○
- ○
- ○
- ○

NOTES & SCRIBBLES

HABITS – 1 NEW PER MONTH
1.
2.
3.

TODAY I'M GRATEFUL FOR

FRIDAY
JANUARY 2023   **13**

TODAY'S PRAYER & FOCUS:

SCHEDULE

TIME	APPOINTMENT

PRIORITIES / GOALS

- ○
- ○
- ○
- ○
- ○
- ○
- ○
- ○
- ○
- ○

NOTES & SCRIBBLES

HABITS – 1 NEW PER MONTH

1.
2.
3.

TODAY I'M GRATEFUL FOR

14 SATURDAY JANUARY 2023

TODAY'S PRAYER & FOCUS:

SCHEDULE

TIME	APPOINTMENT

PRIORITIES / GOALS

- ◯
- ◯
- ◯
- ◯
- ◯
- ◯
- ◯
- ◯
- ◯
- ◯

NOTES & SCRIBBLES

HABITS – 1 NEW PER MONTH

1.
2.
3.

TODAY I'M GRATEFUL FOR

SUNDAY
JANUARY 2023 — **15**

TODAY'S PRAYER & FOCUS:

SCHEDULE

TIME	APPOINTMENT

PRIORITIES / GOALS

- ◯
- ◯
- ◯
- ◯
- ◯
- ◯
- ◯
- ◯
- ◯
- ◯

NOTES & SCRIBBLES

HABITS – 1 NEW PER MONTH

1.
2.
3.

TODAY I'M GRATEFUL FOR

WEEKLY PLANNER

QUOTE OF THE WEEK:

MONDAY 16

TUESDAY 17

WEDNESDAY 18

THURSDAY 19

FRIDAY 20

SATURDAY 21

SUNDAY 22

SUCCESS FOCUS:

PRIORITIES / GOALS

-
-
-
-
-
-
-
-
-

NOTES

JANUARY 16 – 22, 2023

	BREAKFAST	LUNCH	DINNER	SNACKS
M				
T				
W				
T				
F				
S				
S				

SHOPPING LIST:

NOTES

MONDAY
JANUARY 2023
16

TODAY'S PRAYER & FOCUS:

SCHEDULE

TIME	APPOINTMENT

PRIORITIES / GOALS

- ○
- ○
- ○
- ○
- ○
- ○
- ○
- ○
- ○
- ○

NOTES & SCRIBBLES

HABITS – 1 NEW PER MONTH
1.
2.
3.

TODAY I'M GRATEFUL FOR

17

TUESDAY
JANUARY 2023

TODAY'S PRAYER & FOCUS:

SCHEDULE

TIME	APPOINTMENT

PRIORITIES / GOALS

○
○
○
○
○
○
○
○
○
○

NOTES & SCRIBBLES

HABITS – 1 NEW PER MONTH

1.
2.
3.

TODAY I'M GRATEFUL FOR

WEDNESDAY
JANUARY 2023
18

TODAY'S PRAYER & FOCUS:

SCHEDULE

TIME	APPOINTMENT

PRIORITIES / GOALS

- ◯
- ◯
- ◯
- ◯
- ◯
- ◯
- ◯
- ◯
- ◯
- ◯

NOTES & SCRIBBLES

HABITS – 1 NEW PER MONTH

1.
2.
3.

TODAY I'M GRATEFUL FOR

19
THURSDAY
JANUARY 2023

TODAY'S PRAYER & FOCUS:

SCHEDULE

TIME	APPOINTMENT

PRIORITIES / GOALS

- ○
- ○
- ○
- ○
- ○
- ○
- ○
- ○
- ○
- ○

NOTES & SCRIBBLES

HABITS – 1 NEW PER MONTH

1.
2.
3.

TODAY I'M GRATEFUL FOR

FRIDAY
JANUARY 2023
20

TODAY'S PRAYER & FOCUS:

SCHEDULE

TIME	APPOINTMENT

PRIORITIES / GOALS

- ○
- ○
- ○
- ○
- ○
- ○
- ○
- ○
- ○
- ○

NOTES & SCRIBBLES

HABITS – 1 NEW PER MONTH

1.
2.
3.

TODAY I'M GRATEFUL FOR

21

SATURDAY
JANUARY 2023

TODAY'S PRAYER & FOCUS:

SCHEDULE

TIME	APPOINTMENT

PRIORITIES / GOALS

- ○
- ○
- ○
- ○
- ○
- ○
- ○
- ○
- ○
- ○

NOTES & SCRIBBLES

HABITS – 1 NEW PER MONTH

1.
2.
3.

TODAY I'M GRATEFUL FOR

SUNDAY
JANUARY 2023
22

TODAY'S PRAYER & FOCUS:

SCHEDULE

TIME	APPOINTMENT

PRIORITIES / GOALS

- ◯
- ◯
- ◯
- ◯
- ◯
- ◯
- ◯
- ◯
- ◯
- ◯

NOTES & SCRIBBLES

HABITS – 1 NEW PER MONTH

1.
2.
3.

TODAY I'M GRATEFUL FOR

WEEKLY PLANNER

QUOTE OF THE WEEK:

MONDAY 23	
TUESDAY 24	
WEDNESDAY 25	
THURSDAY 26	
FRIDAY 27	
SATURDAY 28	
SUNDAY 29	

SUCCESS FOCUS:

PRIORITIES / GOALS

- ○
- ○
- ○
- ○
- ○
- ○
- ○
- ○
- ○
- ○

NOTES

JANUARY 23 – 29, 2023

	BREAKFAST	LUNCH	DINNER	SNACKS
M				
T				
W				
T				
F				
S				
S				

SHOPPING LIST:

NOTES

MONDAY
JANUARY 2023
23

TODAY'S PRAYER & FOCUS:

SCHEDULE

TIME	APPOINTMENT

PRIORITIES / GOALS

- ○
- ○
- ○
- ○
- ○
- ○
- ○
- ○
- ○
- ○

NOTES & SCRIBBLES

HABITS – 1 NEW PER MONTH

1.
2.
3.

TODAY I'M GRATEFUL FOR

24

TUESDAY
JANUARY 2023

TODAY'S PRAYER & FOCUS:

SCHEDULE

TIME	APPOINTMENT

PRIORITIES / GOALS

- ○
- ○
- ○
- ○
- ○
- ○
- ○
- ○
- ○
- ○

NOTES & SCRIBBLES

HABITS – 1 NEW PER MONTH

1.
2.
3.

TODAY I'M GRATEFUL FOR

WEDNESDAY **25**
JANUARY 2023

TODAY'S PRAYER & FOCUS:

SCHEDULE

TIME	APPOINTMENT

PRIORITIES / GOALS

○
○
○
○
○
○
○
○
○
○

NOTES & SCRIBBLES

HABITS – 1 NEW PER MONTH

1.
2.
3.

TODAY I'M GRATEFUL FOR

26
THURSDAY
JANUARY 2023

TODAY'S PRAYER & FOCUS:

SCHEDULE

TIME	APPOINTMENT

PRIORITIES / GOALS

- ○
- ○
- ○
- ○
- ○
- ○
- ○
- ○
- ○
- ○

NOTES & SCRIBBLES

HABITS – 1 NEW PER MONTH

1.
2.
3.

TODAY I'M GRATEFUL FOR

FRIDAY
JANUARY 2023
27

TODAY'S PRAYER & FOCUS:

SCHEDULE

TIME	APPOINTMENT

PRIORITIES / GOALS

- ○
- ○
- ○
- ○
- ○
- ○
- ○
- ○
- ○
- ○

NOTES & SCRIBBLES

HABITS – 1 NEW PER MONTH

1.
2.
3.

TODAY I'M GRATEFUL FOR

28

SATURDAY
JANUARY 2023

TODAY'S PRAYER & FOCUS:

SCHEDULE

TIME	APPOINTMENT

PRIORITIES / GOALS

- ○
- ○
- ○
- ○
- ○
- ○
- ○
- ○
- ○
- ○

NOTES & SCRIBBLES

HABITS – 1 NEW PER MONTH

1.
2.
3.

TODAY I'M GRATEFUL FOR

SUNDAY
JANUARY 2023
29

TODAY'S PRAYER & FOCUS:

SCHEDULE

TIME	APPOINTMENT

PRIORITIES / GOALS

- ○
- ○
- ○
- ○
- ○
- ○
- ○
- ○
- ○
- ○

NOTES & SCRIBBLES

HABITS – 1 NEW PER MONTH
1.
2.
3.

TODAY I'M GRATEFUL FOR

WEEKLY PLANNER

QUOTE OF THE WEEK:

MONDAY 30	**PRIORITIES / GOALS**
TUESDAY 31	○ _____
WEDNESDAY 1	○ _____
THURSDAY 2	○ _____
FRIDAY 3	○ _____
SATURDAY 4	**NOTES**
SUNDAY 5	
SUCCESS FOCUS:	

JANUARY 30 – FEBRUARY 5, 2023

	BREAKFAST	LUNCH	DINNER	SNACKS
M				
T				
W				
T				
F				
S				
S				

SHOPPING LIST:

NOTES

MONDAY 30
JANUARY 2023

TODAY'S PRAYER & FOCUS:

SCHEDULE

TIME	APPOINTMENT

PRIORITIES / GOALS

- ○
- ○
- ○
- ○
- ○
- ○
- ○
- ○
- ○
- ○

NOTES & SCRIBBLES

HABITS – 1 NEW PER MONTH

1.
2.
3.

TODAY I'M GRATEFUL FOR

31 TUESDAY
JANUARY 2023

TODAY'S PRAYER & FOCUS:

SCHEDULE

TIME	APPOINTMENT

PRIORITIES / GOALS

- ○
- ○
- ○
- ○
- ○
- ○
- ○
- ○
- ○
- ○

NOTES & SCRIBBLES

HABITS – 1 NEW PER MONTH

1.
2.
3.

TODAY I'M GRATEFUL FOR

WEDNESDAY
FEBRUARY 2023

1

TODAY'S PRAYER & FOCUS:

SCHEDULE

TIME	APPOINTMENT

PRIORITIES / GOALS

- ◯
- ◯
- ◯
- ◯
- ◯
- ◯
- ◯
- ◯
- ◯
- ◯

NOTES & SCRIBBLES

HABITS – 1 NEW PER MONTH

1.
2.
3.

TODAY I'M GRATEFUL FOR

2

THURSDAY
FEBRUARY 2023

TODAY'S PRAYER & FOCUS:

SCHEDULE

TIME	APPOINTMENT

PRIORITIES / GOALS

- ○
- ○
- ○
- ○
- ○
- ○
- ○
- ○
- ○
- ○

NOTES & SCRIBBLES

HABITS – 1 NEW PER MONTH

1.
2.
3.

TODAY I'M GRATEFUL FOR

FRIDAY
FEBRUARY 2023
3

TODAY'S PRAYER & FOCUS:

SCHEDULE

TIME	APPOINTMENT

PRIORITIES / GOALS

- ◯
- ◯
- ◯
- ◯
- ◯
- ◯
- ◯
- ◯
- ◯
- ◯

NOTES & SCRIBBLES

HABITS – 1 NEW PER MONTH

1.
2.
3.

TODAY I'M GRATEFUL FOR

4

SATURDAY
FEBRUARY 2023

TODAY'S PRAYER & FOCUS:

SCHEDULE

TIME	APPOINTMENT

PRIORITIES / GOALS

- ○
- ○
- ○
- ○
- ○
- ○
- ○
- ○
- ○
- ○

NOTES & SCRIBBLES

HABITS – 1 NEW PER MONTH

1.
2.
3.

TODAY I'M GRATEFUL FOR

SUNDAY
FEBRUARY 2023

5

TODAY'S PRAYER & FOCUS:

SCHEDULE

TIME	APPOINTMENT

PRIORITIES / GOALS

- ○
- ○
- ○
- ○
- ○
- ○
- ○
- ○
- ○
- ○

NOTES & SCRIBBLES

HABITS – 1 NEW PER MONTH

1.
2.
3.

TODAY I'M GRATEFUL FOR

JANUARY 2023 INCOME TRACKER

DATE	INCOME	CATEGORY	AMOUNT
TOTAL			

JANUARY 2023 EXPENSE TRACKER

DATE	EXPENSE	CATEGORY	AMOUNT
TOTAL			

JANUARY 2023 SAVINGS TRACKER

SAVING FOR: _____ GOAL AMOUNT: _____

DATE	NOTES	AMOUNT	BALANCE
TOTAL			

MONTHLY PROGRESS - JANUARY 2023

I HAVE ACHIEVED...

I AM THANKFUL...

I'D LIKE TO IMPROVE...

HOW I WILL CELEBRATE WHAT I DID WELL...

FEBRUARY

MONDAY	TUESDAY	WEDNESDAY	THURSDAY
		1	2
6	7	8	9
13	14	15	16
20	21	22	23
27	28		

GOALS

2023

FRIDAY	SATURDAY	SUNDAY	NOTES
3	4	5	
10	11	12	
17	18	19	
24	25	26	

NOTES

MASTER SUCCESS ACTIONS
FEBRUARY 2023

List 4 life areas and your goals to focus on this month:

1.

2.

3.

4.

Use this master task list for the big action steps you will commit to do this month. They will accomplish the goals you set to improve your life in the 4 areas of focus. Your daily tasks will be the small steps to accomplish these bigger steps.

DONE	SUCCESS ACTIONS

NOTES

WEEKLY PLANNER

QUOTE OF THE WEEK:

MONDAY 6	
TUESDAY 7	
WEDNESDAY 8	
THURSDAY 9	
FRIDAY 10	
SATURDAY 11	
SUNDAY 12	

SUCCESS FOCUS:

PRIORITIES / GOALS

○
○
○
○
○
○
○
○
○
○

NOTES

FEBRUARY 6 – 12, 2023

	BREAKFAST	LUNCH	DINNER	SNACKS
M				
T				
W				
T				
F				
S				
S				

SHOPPING LIST:

NOTES

MONDAY
FEBRUARY 2023

6

TODAY'S PRAYER & FOCUS:

SCHEDULE

TIME	APPOINTMENT

PRIORITIES / GOALS

- ◯
- ◯
- ◯
- ◯
- ◯
- ◯
- ◯
- ◯
- ◯
- ◯

NOTES & SCRIBBLES

HABITS – 1 NEW PER MONTH

1.
2.
3.

TODAY I'M GRATEFUL FOR

7

TUESDAY
FEBRUARY 2023

TODAY'S PRAYER & FOCUS:

SCHEDULE

TIME	APPOINTMENT

PRIORITIES / GOALS

- ○
- ○
- ○
- ○
- ○
- ○
- ○
- ○
- ○
- ○

NOTES & SCRIBBLES

HABITS – 1 NEW PER MONTH

1.
2.
3.

TODAY I'M GRATEFUL FOR

WEDNESDAY
FEBRUARY 2023

8

TODAY'S PRAYER & FOCUS:

SCHEDULE

TIME	APPOINTMENT

PRIORITIES / GOALS

- ◯
- ◯
- ◯
- ◯
- ◯
- ◯
- ◯
- ◯
- ◯
- ◯

NOTES & SCRIBBLES

HABITS – 1 NEW PER MONTH

1.
2.
3.

TODAY I'M GRATEFUL FOR

9

THURSDAY
FEBRUARY 2023

TODAY'S PRAYER & FOCUS:

SCHEDULE

TIME	APPOINTMENT

PRIORITIES / GOALS

- ◯
- ◯
- ◯
- ◯
- ◯
- ◯
- ◯
- ◯
- ◯
- ◯

NOTES & SCRIBBLES

HABITS – 1 NEW PER MONTH
1.
2.
3.

TODAY I'M GRATEFUL FOR

FRIDAY
FEBRUARY 2023
10

TODAY'S PRAYER & FOCUS:

SCHEDULE

TIME	APPOINTMENT

PRIORITIES / GOALS

- ○
- ○
- ○
- ○
- ○
- ○
- ○
- ○
- ○
- ○

NOTES & SCRIBBLES

HABITS – 1 NEW PER MONTH
1.
2.
3.

TODAY I'M GRATEFUL FOR

11
SATURDAY
FEBRUARY 2023

TODAY'S PRAYER & FOCUS:

SCHEDULE

TIME	APPOINTMENT

PRIORITIES / GOALS

- ○
- ○
- ○
- ○
- ○
- ○
- ○
- ○
- ○
- ○

NOTES & SCRIBBLES

HABITS – 1 NEW PER MONTH
1.
2.
3.

TODAY I'M GRATEFUL FOR

SUNDAY
FEBRUARY 2023
12

TODAY'S PRAYER & FOCUS:

SCHEDULE

TIME	APPOINTMENT

PRIORITIES / GOALS

- ○
- ○
- ○
- ○
- ○
- ○
- ○
- ○
- ○
- ○

NOTES & SCRIBBLES

HABITS – 1 NEW PER MONTH

1.
2.
3.

TODAY I'M GRATEFUL FOR

WEEKLY PLANNER

QUOTE OF THE WEEK:

MONDAY 13	
TUESDAY 14	
WEDNESDAY 15	
THURSDAY 16	
FRIDAY 17	
SATURDAY 18	
SUNDAY 19	

SUCCESS FOCUS:

PRIORITIES / GOALS

- ○
- ○
- ○
- ○
- ○
- ○
- ○
- ○
- ○
- ○

NOTES

FEBRUARY 13 – 19, 2023

	BREAKFAST	LUNCH	DINNER	SNACKS
M				
T				
W				
T				
F				
S				
S				

SHOPPING LIST:

NOTES

MONDAY
FEBRUARY 2023
13

TODAY'S PRAYER & FOCUS:

SCHEDULE

TIME	APPOINTMENT

PRIORITIES / GOALS

- ◯
- ◯
- ◯
- ◯
- ◯
- ◯
- ◯
- ◯
- ◯
- ◯

NOTES & SCRIBBLES

HABITS – 1 NEW PER MONTH

1.
2.
3.

TODAY I'M GRATEFUL FOR

14

TUESDAY
FEBRUARY 2023

TODAY'S PRAYER & FOCUS:

SCHEDULE

TIME	APPOINTMENT

PRIORITIES / GOALS

- ◯
- ◯
- ◯
- ◯
- ◯
- ◯
- ◯
- ◯
- ◯
- ◯

NOTES & SCRIBBLES

HABITS – 1 NEW PER MONTH

1.
2.
3.

TODAY I'M GRATEFUL FOR

WEDNESDAY
FEBRUARY 2023
15

TODAY'S PRAYER & FOCUS:

SCHEDULE

TIME	APPOINTMENT

PRIORITIES / GOALS

- ◯
- ◯
- ◯
- ◯
- ◯
- ◯
- ◯
- ◯
- ◯
- ◯

NOTES & SCRIBBLES

HABITS – 1 NEW PER MONTH

1.
2.
3.

TODAY I'M GRATEFUL FOR

16
THURSDAY
FEBRUARY 2023

TODAY'S PRAYER & FOCUS:

SCHEDULE

TIME	APPOINTMENT

PRIORITIES / GOALS

- ○
- ○
- ○
- ○
- ○
- ○
- ○
- ○
- ○
- ○

NOTES & SCRIBBLES

HABITS – 1 NEW PER MONTH

1.
2.
3.

TODAY I'M GRATEFUL FOR

FRIDAY
FEBRUARY 2023
17

TODAY'S PRAYER & FOCUS:

SCHEDULE

TIME	APPOINTMENT

PRIORITIES / GOALS

○
○
○
○
○
○
○
○
○
○

NOTES & SCRIBBLES

HABITS – 1 NEW PER MONTH

1.
2.
3.

TODAY I'M GRATEFUL FOR

18

SATURDAY
FEBRUARY 2023

TODAY'S PRAYER & FOCUS:

SCHEDULE

TIME	APPOINTMENT

PRIORITIES / GOALS

- ◯
- ◯
- ◯
- ◯
- ◯
- ◯
- ◯
- ◯
- ◯
- ◯

NOTES & SCRIBBLES

HABITS – 1 NEW PER MONTH

1.
2.
3.

TODAY I'M GRATEFUL FOR

SUNDAY
FEBRUARY 2023
19

TODAY'S PRAYER & FOCUS:

SCHEDULE

TIME	APPOINTMENT

PRIORITIES / GOALS

- ○
- ○
- ○
- ○
- ○
- ○
- ○
- ○
- ○
- ○

NOTES & SCRIBBLES

HABITS – 1 NEW PER MONTH

1.
2.
3.

TODAY I'M GRATEFUL FOR

WEEKLY PLANNER

QUOTE OF THE WEEK:

MONDAY 20	
TUESDAY 21	
WEDNESDAY 22	
THURSDAY 23	
FRIDAY 24	
SATURDAY 25	
SUNDAY 26	

SUCCESS FOCUS:

PRIORITIES / GOALS

○
○
○
○
○
○
○
○
○
○

NOTES

FEBRUARY 20 – 26, 2023

	BREAKFAST	LUNCH	DINNER	SNACKS
M				
T				
W				
T				
F				
S				
S				

SHOPPING LIST:

NOTES

MONDAY
FEBRUARY 2023 — 20

TODAY'S PRAYER & FOCUS:

SCHEDULE

TIME	APPOINTMENT

PRIORITIES / GOALS

- ○
- ○
- ○
- ○
- ○
- ○
- ○
- ○
- ○
- ○

NOTES & SCRIBBLES

HABITS – 1 NEW PER MONTH

1.
2.
3.

TODAY I'M GRATEFUL FOR

21
TUESDAY
FEBRUARY 2023

TODAY'S PRAYER & FOCUS:

SCHEDULE

TIME	APPOINTMENT

PRIORITIES / GOALS

- ○
- ○
- ○
- ○
- ○
- ○
- ○
- ○
- ○
- ○

NOTES & SCRIBBLES

HABITS – 1 NEW PER MONTH

1.
2.
3.

TODAY I'M GRATEFUL FOR

WEDNESDAY
FEBRUARY 2023

22

TODAY'S PRAYER & FOCUS:

SCHEDULE

TIME	APPOINTMENT

PRIORITIES / GOALS

- ○
- ○
- ○
- ○
- ○
- ○
- ○
- ○
- ○
- ○

NOTES & SCRIBBLES

HABITS – 1 NEW PER MONTH

1.
2.
3.

TODAY I'M GRATEFUL FOR

23 THURSDAY FEBRUARY 2023

TODAY'S PRAYER & FOCUS:

SCHEDULE

TIME	APPOINTMENT

PRIORITIES / GOALS

- ○
- ○
- ○
- ○
- ○
- ○
- ○
- ○
- ○
- ○

NOTES & SCRIBBLES

HABITS – 1 NEW PER MONTH

1.
2.
3.

TODAY I'M GRATEFUL FOR

FRIDAY
FEBRUARY 2023
24

TODAY'S PRAYER & FOCUS:

SCHEDULE

TIME	APPOINTMENT

PRIORITIES / GOALS

- ○
- ○
- ○
- ○
- ○
- ○
- ○
- ○
- ○

NOTES & SCRIBBLES

HABITS – 1 NEW PER MONTH

1.
2.
3.

TODAY I'M GRATEFUL FOR

25 SATURDAY
FEBRUARY 2023

TODAY'S PRAYER & FOCUS:

SCHEDULE

TIME	APPOINTMENT

PRIORITIES / GOALS

- ◯
- ◯
- ◯
- ◯
- ◯
- ◯
- ◯
- ◯
- ◯
- ◯

NOTES & SCRIBBLES

HABITS — 1 NEW PER MONTH
1.
2.
3.

TODAY I'M GRATEFUL FOR

SUNDAY
FEBRUARY 2023
26

TODAY'S PRAYER & FOCUS:

SCHEDULE

TIME	APPOINTMENT

PRIORITIES / GOALS

- ○
- ○
- ○
- ○
- ○
- ○
- ○
- ○
- ○
- ○

NOTES & SCRIBBLES

HABITS – 1 NEW PER MONTH

1.
2.
3.

TODAY I'M GRATEFUL FOR

WEEKLY PLANNER

QUOTE OF THE WEEK:

MONDAY 27
TUESDAY 28
WEDNESDAY 1
THURSDAY 2
FRIDAY 3
SATURDAY 4
SUNDAY 5

SUCCESS FOCUS:

PRIORITIES / GOALS

-
-
-
-
-
-
-
-
-

NOTES

FEBRUARY 27 – MARCH 5, 2023

	BREAKFAST	LUNCH	DINNER	SNACKS
M				
T				
W				
T				
F				
S				
S				

SHOPPING LIST:

NOTES

MONDAY
FEBRUARY 2023
27

TODAY'S PRAYER & FOCUS:

SCHEDULE

TIME	APPOINTMENT

PRIORITIES / GOALS

- ○
- ○
- ○
- ○
- ○
- ○
- ○
- ○
- ○
- ○

NOTES & SCRIBBLES

HABITS – 1 NEW PER MONTH
1.
2.
3.

TODAY I'M GRATEFUL FOR

28 TUESDAY
FEBRUARY 2023

TODAY'S PRAYER & FOCUS:

SCHEDULE

TIME	APPOINTMENT

PRIORITIES / GOALS

- ○
- ○
- ○
- ○
- ○
- ○
- ○
- ○
- ○
- ○

NOTES & SCRIBBLES

HABITS – 1 NEW PER MONTH

1.
2.
3.

TODAY I'M GRATEFUL FOR

WEDNESDAY
MARCH 2023

1

TODAY'S PRAYER & FOCUS:

SCHEDULE

TIME	APPOINTMENT

PRIORITIES / GOALS

- ○
- ○
- ○
- ○
- ○
- ○
- ○
- ○
- ○
- ○

NOTES & SCRIBBLES

HABITS – 1 NEW PER MONTH

1.
2.
3.

TODAY I'M GRATEFUL FOR

2

THURSDAY
MARCH 2023

TODAY'S PRAYER & FOCUS:

SCHEDULE

TIME	APPOINTMENT

PRIORITIES / GOALS

- ○
- ○
- ○
- ○
- ○
- ○
- ○
- ○
- ○
- ○

NOTES & SCRIBBLES

HABITS – 1 NEW PER MONTH

1.
2.
3.

TODAY I'M GRATEFUL FOR

FRIDAY
MARCH 2023
3

TODAY'S PRAYER & FOCUS:

SCHEDULE

TIME	APPOINTMENT

PRIORITIES / GOALS

- ◯
- ◯
- ◯
- ◯
- ◯
- ◯
- ◯
- ◯
- ◯
- ◯

NOTES & SCRIBBLES

HABITS – 1 NEW PER MONTH
1.
2.
3.

TODAY I'M GRATEFUL FOR

4

SATURDAY
MARCH 2023

TODAY'S PRAYER & FOCUS:

SCHEDULE

TIME	APPOINTMENT

PRIORITIES / GOALS

- ◯
- ◯
- ◯
- ◯
- ◯
- ◯
- ◯
- ◯
- ◯
- ◯

NOTES & SCRIBBLES

HABITS – 1 NEW PER MONTH

1.
2.
3.

TODAY I'M GRATEFUL FOR

SUNDAY
MARCH 2023

5

TODAY'S PRAYER & FOCUS:

SCHEDULE

TIME	APPOINTMENT

PRIORITIES / GOALS

- ○
- ○
- ○
- ○
- ○
- ○
- ○
- ○
- ○
- ○

NOTES & SCRIBBLES

HABITS – 1 NEW PER MONTH

1.
2.
3.

TODAY I'M GRATEFUL FOR

FEBRUARY 2023 INCOME TRACKER

DATE	INCOME	CATEGORY	AMOUNT
TOTAL			

FEBRUARY 2023 EXPENSE TRACKER

DATE	EXPENSE	CATEGORY	AMOUNT
TOTAL			

FEBRUARY 2023 SAVINGS TRACKER

SAVING FOR: _____   GOAL AMOUNT: _____

DATE	NOTES	AMOUNT	BALANCE
TOTAL			

MONTHLY PROGRESS - FEBRUARY 2023

I HAVE ACHIEVED...

I AM THANKFUL...

I'D LIKE TO IMPROVE...

HOW I WILL CELEBRATE WHAT I DID WELL...

MARCH

MONDAY	TUESDAY	WEDNESDAY	THURSDAY
		1	2
6	7	8	9
13	14	15	16
20	21	22	23
27	28	29	30

GOALS

2023

FRIDAY	SATURDAY	SUNDAY	NOTES
3	4	5	
10	11	12	
17	18	19	
24	25	26	
31			

NOTES

MASTER SUCCESS ACTIONS
MARCH 2023

List 4 life areas and your goals to focus on this month:

1.

2.

3.

4.

Use this master task list for the big action steps you will commit to do this month. They will accomplish the goals you set to improve your life in the 4 areas of focus. Your daily tasks will be the small steps to accomplish these bigger steps.

DONE	SUCCESS ACTIONS

NOTES

WEEKLY PLANNER

QUOTE OF THE WEEK:

MONDAY 6

TUESDAY 7

WEDNESDAY 8

THURSDAY 9

FRIDAY 10

SATURDAY 11

SUNDAY 12

PRIORITIES / GOALS

- ○
- ○
- ○
- ○
- ○
- ○
- ○
- ○
- ○
- ○

NOTES

SUCCESS FOCUS:

MARCH 6 – 12, 2023

	BREAKFAST	LUNCH	DINNER	SNACKS
M				
T				
W				
T				
F				
S				
S				

SHOPPING LIST:

NOTES

MONDAY
MARCH 2023
6

TODAY'S PRAYER & FOCUS:

SCHEDULE

TIME	APPOINTMENT

PRIORITIES / GOALS

- ○
- ○
- ○
- ○
- ○
- ○
- ○
- ○
- ○
- ○

NOTES & SCRIBBLES

HABITS – 1 NEW PER MONTH

1.
2.
3.

TODAY I'M GRATEFUL FOR

7

TUESDAY
MARCH 2023

TODAY'S PRAYER & FOCUS:

SCHEDULE

TIME	APPOINTMENT

PRIORITIES / GOALS

- ○
- ○
- ○
- ○
- ○
- ○
- ○
- ○
- ○
- ○

NOTES & SCRIBBLES

HABITS – 1 NEW PER MONTH

1.
2.
3.

TODAY I'M GRATEFUL FOR

WEDNESDAY
MARCH 2023

8

TODAY'S PRAYER & FOCUS:

SCHEDULE

TIME	APPOINTMENT

PRIORITIES / GOALS

- ◯
- ◯
- ◯
- ◯
- ◯
- ◯
- ◯
- ◯
- ◯
- ◯

NOTES & SCRIBBLES

HABITS – 1 NEW PER MONTH
1.
2.
3.

TODAY I'M GRATEFUL FOR

9

THURSDAY
MARCH 2023

TODAY'S PRAYER & FOCUS:

SCHEDULE

TIME	APPOINTMENT

PRIORITIES / GOALS

- ○
- ○
- ○
- ○
- ○
- ○
- ○
- ○
- ○
- ○

NOTES & SCRIBBLES

HABITS – 1 NEW PER MONTH

1.
2.
3.

TODAY I'M GRATEFUL FOR

FRIDAY
MARCH 2023 **10**

TODAY'S PRAYER & FOCUS:

SCHEDULE

TIME	APPOINTMENT

PRIORITIES / GOALS

- ○
- ○
- ○
- ○
- ○
- ○
- ○
- ○
- ○

NOTES & SCRIBBLES

HABITS – 1 NEW PER MONTH
1.
2.
3.

TODAY I'M GRATEFUL FOR

11

SATURDAY
MARCH 2023

TODAY'S PRAYER & FOCUS:

SCHEDULE

TIME	APPOINTMENT

PRIORITIES / GOALS

- ○
- ○
- ○
- ○
- ○
- ○
- ○
- ○
- ○
- ○

NOTES & SCRIBBLES

HABITS – 1 NEW PER MONTH

1.
2.
3.

TODAY I'M GRATEFUL FOR

SUNDAY
MARCH 2023 **12**

TODAY'S PRAYER & FOCUS:

SCHEDULE

TIME	APPOINTMENT

PRIORITIES / GOALS

- ◯
- ◯
- ◯
- ◯
- ◯
- ◯
- ◯
- ◯
- ◯
- ◯

NOTES & SCRIBBLES

HABITS – 1 NEW PER MONTH

1.
2.
3.

TODAY I'M GRATEFUL FOR

WEEKLY PLANNER

QUOTE OF THE WEEK:

MONDAY 13	
TUESDAY 14	
WEDNESDAY 15	
THURSDAY 16	
FRIDAY 17	
SATURDAY 18	
SUNDAY 19	

PRIORITIES / GOALS

○
○
○
○
○
○
○
○
○
○

NOTES

SUCCESS FOCUS:

MARCH 13 – 19, 2023

	BREAKFAST	LUNCH	DINNER	SNACKS
M				
T				
W				
T				
F				
S				
S				

SHOPPING LIST:

NOTES

MONDAY
MARCH 2023
13

TODAY'S PRAYER & FOCUS:

SCHEDULE

TIME	APPOINTMENT

PRIORITIES / GOALS

○
○
○
○
○
○
○
○
○
○

NOTES & SCRIBBLES

HABITS – 1 NEW PER MONTH

1.
2.
3.

TODAY I'M GRATEFUL FOR

14

TUESDAY
MARCH 2023

TODAY'S PRAYER & FOCUS:

SCHEDULE

TIME	APPOINTMENT

PRIORITIES / GOALS

- ◯
- ◯
- ◯
- ◯
- ◯
- ◯
- ◯
- ◯
- ◯
- ◯

NOTES & SCRIBBLES

HABITS – 1 NEW PER MONTH

1.
2.
3.

TODAY I'M GRATEFUL FOR

WEDNESDAY
MARCH 2023
15

TODAY'S PRAYER & FOCUS:

SCHEDULE

TIME	APPOINTMENT

PRIORITIES / GOALS

- ○
- ○
- ○
- ○
- ○
- ○
- ○
- ○
- ○

NOTES & SCRIBBLES

HABITS – 1 NEW PER MONTH
1.
2.
3.

TODAY I'M GRATEFUL FOR

16

THURSDAY
MARCH 2023

TODAY'S PRAYER & FOCUS:

SCHEDULE

TIME	APPOINTMENT

PRIORITIES / GOALS

- ◯
- ◯
- ◯
- ◯
- ◯
- ◯
- ◯
- ◯
- ◯
- ◯

NOTES & SCRIBBLES

HABITS — 1 NEW PER MONTH

1.
2.
3.

TODAY I'M GRATEFUL FOR

FRIDAY
MARCH 2023
17

TODAY'S PRAYER & FOCUS:

SCHEDULE

TIME	APPOINTMENT

PRIORITIES / GOALS

- ○
- ○
- ○
- ○
- ○
- ○
- ○
- ○
- ○
- ○

NOTES & SCRIBBLES

HABITS – 1 NEW PER MONTH

1.
2.
3.

TODAY I'M GRATEFUL FOR

18
SATURDAY
MARCH 2023

TODAY'S PRAYER & FOCUS:

SCHEDULE

TIME	APPOINTMENT

PRIORITIES / GOALS

- ○
- ○
- ○
- ○
- ○
- ○
- ○
- ○
- ○
- ○

NOTES & SCRIBBLES

HABITS – 1 NEW PER MONTH

1.
2.
3.

TODAY I'M GRATEFUL FOR

SUNDAY
MARCH 2023 **19**

TODAY'S PRAYER & FOCUS:

SCHEDULE

TIME	APPOINTMENT

PRIORITIES / GOALS

- ◯
- ◯
- ◯
- ◯
- ◯
- ◯
- ◯
- ◯
- ◯
- ◯

NOTES & SCRIBBLES

HABITS – 1 NEW PER MONTH

1.
2.
3.

TODAY I'M GRATEFUL FOR

WEEKLY PLANNER

QUOTE OF THE WEEK:

MONDAY 20
TUESDAY 21
WEDNESDAY 22
THURSDAY 23
FRIDAY 24
SATURDAY 25
SUNDAY 26

SUCCESS FOCUS:

PRIORITIES / GOALS

○
○
○
○
○
○
○
○
○
○

NOTES

MARCH 20 – 26, 2023

	BREAKFAST	LUNCH	DINNER	SNACKS
M				
T				
W				
T				
F				
S				
S				

SHOPPING LIST:

NOTES

MONDAY
MARCH 2023 — 20

TODAY'S PRAYER & FOCUS:

SCHEDULE

TIME	APPOINTMENT

PRIORITIES / GOALS

- ◯
- ◯
- ◯
- ◯
- ◯
- ◯
- ◯
- ◯
- ◯
- ◯

NOTES & SCRIBBLES

HABITS – 1 NEW PER MONTH

1.
2.
3.

TODAY I'M GRATEFUL FOR

21

TUESDAY
MARCH 2023

TODAY'S PRAYER & FOCUS:

SCHEDULE

TIME	APPOINTMENT

PRIORITIES / GOALS

- ◯
- ◯
- ◯
- ◯
- ◯
- ◯
- ◯
- ◯
- ◯
- ◯

NOTES & SCRIBBLES

HABITS – 1 NEW PER MONTH

1.
2.
3.

TODAY I'M GRATEFUL FOR

WEDNESDAY
MARCH 2023
22

TODAY'S PRAYER & FOCUS:

SCHEDULE

TIME	APPOINTMENT

PRIORITIES / GOALS

- ○
- ○
- ○
- ○
- ○
- ○
- ○
- ○
- ○
- ○

NOTES & SCRIBBLES

HABITS – 1 NEW PER MONTH

1.
2.
3.

TODAY I'M GRATEFUL FOR

23 THURSDAY
MARCH 2023

TODAY'S PRAYER & FOCUS:

SCHEDULE

TIME	APPOINTMENT

PRIORITIES / GOALS

- ○
- ○
- ○
- ○
- ○
- ○
- ○
- ○
- ○
- ○

NOTES & SCRIBBLES

HABITS – 1 NEW PER MONTH

1.
2.
3.

TODAY I'M GRATEFUL FOR

FRIDAY
MARCH 2023
24

TODAY'S PRAYER & FOCUS:

SCHEDULE

TIME	APPOINTMENT

PRIORITIES / GOALS

- ◯
- ◯
- ◯
- ◯
- ◯
- ◯
- ◯
- ◯
- ◯
- ◯

NOTES & SCRIBBLES

HABITS – 1 NEW PER MONTH

1.
2.
3.

TODAY I'M GRATEFUL FOR

25
SATURDAY
MARCH 2023

TODAY'S PRAYER & FOCUS:

SCHEDULE

TIME	APPOINTMENT

PRIORITIES / GOALS

- ○
- ○
- ○
- ○
- ○
- ○
- ○
- ○
- ○
- ○

NOTES & SCRIBBLES

HABITS – 1 NEW PER MONTH

1.
2.
3.

TODAY I'M GRATEFUL FOR

SUNDAY
MARCH 2023 — 26

TODAY'S PRAYER & FOCUS:

SCHEDULE

TIME	APPOINTMENT

PRIORITIES / GOALS

- ○
- ○
- ○
- ○
- ○
- ○
- ○
- ○
- ○
- ○

NOTES & SCRIBBLES

HABITS – 1 NEW PER MONTH
1.
2.
3.

TODAY I'M GRATEFUL FOR

WEEKLY PLANNER

QUOTE OF THE WEEK:

MONDAY 27
TUESDAY 28
WEDNESDAY 29
THURSDAY 30
FRIDAY 31
SATURDAY 1
SUNDAY 2

SUCCESS FOCUS:

PRIORITIES / GOALS

- ○
- ○
- ○
- ○
- ○
- ○
- ○
- ○
- ○
- ○

NOTES

MARCH 27 – APRIL 2, 2023

	BREAKFAST	LUNCH	DINNER	SNACKS
M				
T				
W				
T				
F				
S				
S				

SHOPPING LIST:

NOTES

MONDAY
MARCH 2023
27

TODAY'S PRAYER & FOCUS:

SCHEDULE

TIME	APPOINTMENT

PRIORITIES / GOALS

- ○
- ○
- ○
- ○
- ○
- ○
- ○
- ○
- ○
- ○

NOTES & SCRIBBLES

HABITS – 1 NEW PER MONTH

1.
2.
3.

TODAY I'M GRATEFUL FOR

28

TUESDAY
MARCH 2023

TODAY'S PRAYER & FOCUS:

SCHEDULE

TIME	APPOINTMENT

PRIORITIES / GOALS

- ○
- ○
- ○
- ○
- ○
- ○
- ○
- ○
- ○
- ○

NOTES & SCRIBBLES

HABITS – 1 NEW PER MONTH

1.
2.
3.

TODAY I'M GRATEFUL FOR

**WEDNESDAY
MARCH 2023** **29**

TODAY'S PRAYER & FOCUS:

SCHEDULE

TIME	APPOINTMENT

PRIORITIES / GOALS

- ○
- ○
- ○
- ○
- ○
- ○
- ○
- ○
- ○
- ○

NOTES & SCRIBBLES

HABITS – 1 NEW PER MONTH

1.
2.
3.

TODAY I'M GRATEFUL FOR

30 THURSDAY MARCH 2023

TODAY'S PRAYER & FOCUS:

SCHEDULE

TIME	APPOINTMENT

PRIORITIES / GOALS

- ○
- ○
- ○
- ○
- ○
- ○
- ○
- ○
- ○
- ○

NOTES & SCRIBBLES

HABITS – 1 NEW PER MONTH

1.
2.
3.

TODAY I'M GRATEFUL FOR

FRIDAY
MARCH 2023
31

TODAY'S PRAYER & FOCUS:

SCHEDULE

TIME	APPOINTMENT

PRIORITIES / GOALS

- ◯
- ◯
- ◯
- ◯
- ◯
- ◯
- ◯
- ◯
- ◯
- ◯

NOTES & SCRIBBLES

HABITS – 1 NEW PER MONTH

1.
2.
3.

TODAY I'M GRATEFUL FOR

1

SATURDAY
APRIL 2023

TODAY'S PRAYER & FOCUS:

SCHEDULE

TIME	APPOINTMENT

PRIORITIES / GOALS

- ○
- ○
- ○
- ○
- ○
- ○
- ○
- ○
- ○
- ○

NOTES & SCRIBBLES

HABITS – 1 NEW PER MONTH

1.
2.
3.

TODAY I'M GRATEFUL FOR

SUNDAY
APRIL 2023
2

TODAY'S PRAYER & FOCUS:

SCHEDULE

TIME	APPOINTMENT

PRIORITIES / GOALS

- ○
- ○
- ○
- ○
- ○
- ○
- ○
- ○
- ○
- ○

NOTES & SCRIBBLES

HABITS – 1 NEW PER MONTH

1.
2.
3.

TODAY I'M GRATEFUL FOR

MARCH 2023 INCOME TRACKER

DATE	INCOME	CATEGORY	AMOUNT
TOTAL			

MARCH 2023 EXPENSE TRACKER

DATE	EXPENSE	CATEGORY	AMOUNT
TOTAL			

MARCH 2023 SAVINGS TRACKER

SAVING FOR: _____ **GOAL AMOUNT:** _____

DATE	NOTES	AMOUNT	BALANCE
TOTAL			

MONTHLY PROGRESS - MARCH 2023

I HAVE ACHIEVED...

I AM THANKFUL...

I'D LIKE TO IMPROVE...

HOW I WILL CELEBRATE WHAT I DID WELL...

BOOKS TO READ

TITLE	AUTHOR	✓

WISH LIST

PRODUCT	PRICE	STORE

NOTES

NOTES

NOTES

NOTES

NOTES

NOTES

NOTES

NOTES

NOTES

NOTES

NOTES

NOTES

NOTES

NOTES

NOTES

NOTES

NOTES

NOTES

NOTES

NOTES

INDEX

TOPIC	PAGE(S)

INDEX

TOPIC	PAGE(S)

INDEX

TOPIC	PAGE(S)

INDEX

TOPIC	PAGE(S)

www.ingramcontent.com/pod-product-compliance
Lightning Source LLC
Chambersburg PA
CBHW071742150426
43191CB00010B/1661